I love reading

Dinosaur World

Flying Giants

by Monica Hughes

Consultant: Dougal Dixon

ticktock

Copyright © **ticktock Entertainment Ltd 2007**
First published in Great Britain in 2007 by **ticktock Media Ltd.,**
Unit 2, Orchard Business Centre, North Farm Road, Tunbridge Wells, Kent TN2 3XF

We would like to thank: Shirley Bickler and Suzanne Baker

ISBN 978 1 84696 604 0 pbk
Printed in China

Picture credits
t=top, b=bottom, c=centre, l-left, r=right, OFC= outside front cover
Lisa Alderson: 8-9, 12b; Simon Mendez: 4, 5, 12t; NHM: 6; Shutterstock: 8, 12, 15b,
16, 23b; Luis Rey: 1, 6-7, 10-11, 14-15, 17, 18-19, 20, 21, , 22t, 22b, 23t, 23c.

CONTENTS

Very old creatures

These flying creatures lived long before the dinosaurs lived.

Coelurosauravus
see-lo-ro-sor-a-vus

This one looked like a lizard but with wings made of skin.

This one looked like a dragonfly, but it was much bigger. It was as big as a seagull.

Meganeura
meg-an-ura

The pterosaurs

The pterosaurs lived at the time of the dinosaurs.

They were big flying animals.

Pterosaur
terr-o-sor

Some of them had long tails and narrow wings.

Some had short tails and wide wings.

Narrow wings

This pterosaur had narrow wings and a long tail. It ate insects.

Long tail

Insect

Furry body

It had a furry body.

Sordes
sor-dees

It had a
long mouth
and a few
sharp teeth.

Wings

9

Furry body

This pterosaur was one metre from wing tip to wing tip.

It had a furry body and long narrow wings and a long tail.

It liked to eat fish.

Long tail

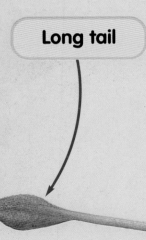

Eudimorphodon
you-dee-morf-o-don

It had two different
kinds of teeth.

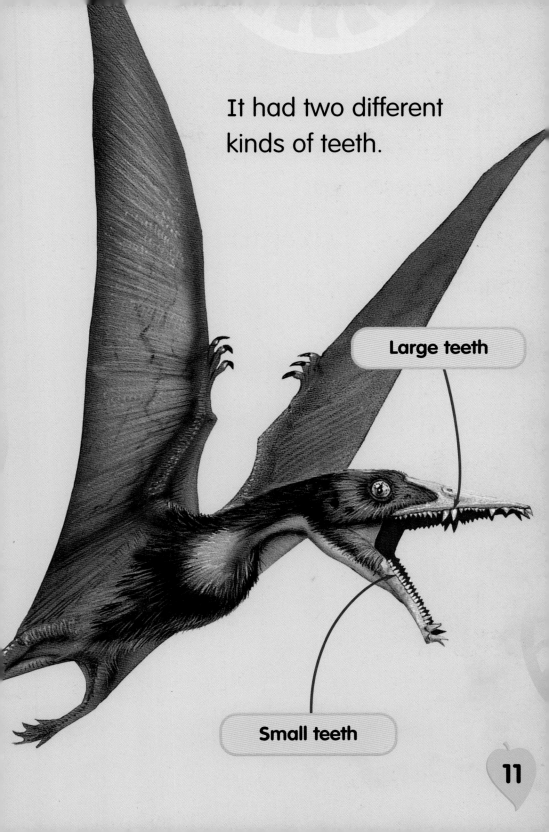

Large teeth

Small teeth

Big head

This pterosaur had a long tail and narrow wings.

Dimorphodon
die-morf-o-don

It had two kinds of teeth and ate fish.

Fish

It had a very big head and
a colourful beak.

13

Short tail

Pterodactylus
terr-o-dack-till-us

This flying animal was
one metre from wing tip
to wing tip.

It had a short tail
and big wide wings.

It had lots of teeth and
ate fish and small lizards.

Wide wings

Lizard

Colourful crest

This pterosaur was three metres from wing tip to wing tip.

It had pointed jaws and it ate shellfish.

Shellfish

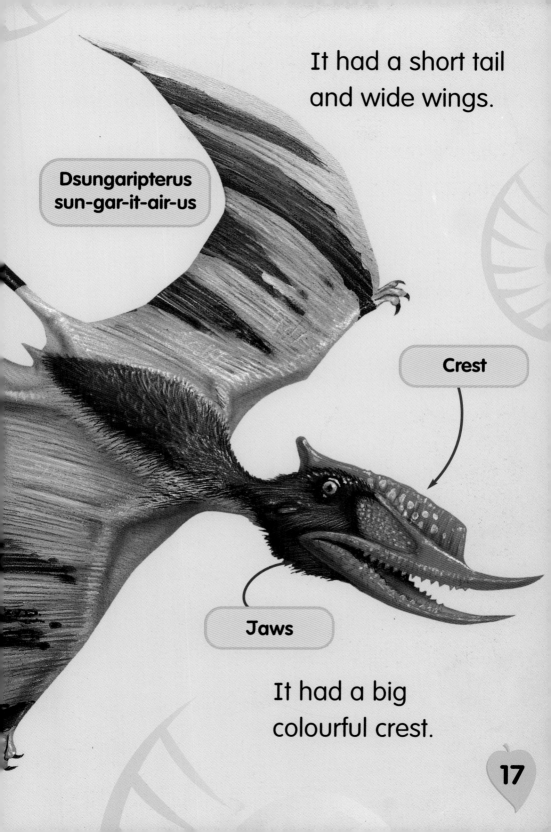

It had a short tail and wide wings.

Dsungaripterus
sun-gar-it-air-us

Crest

Jaws

It had a big colourful crest.

17

As big as a plane

This pterosaur was as big as a small aeroplane.

It was about 11 metres from wing tip to wing tip.

It had a long neck and very long jaws.

It ate dead dinosaurs.

Quetzalcoatlus
ket-sal-koat-lus

Jaws

Neck

The first bird

We think this is what the first bird looked like.

It did not have a beak but a jaw and teeth like a dinosaur.

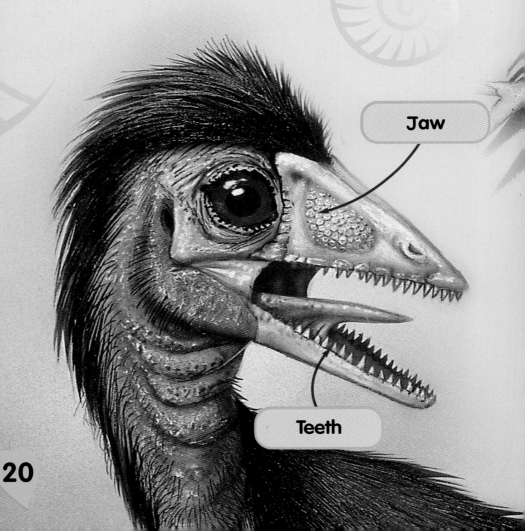

Jaw

Teeth

Archaeopteryx
ark-ee-op-ter-ix

Feathers

It had feathers like a bird.

It had a long tail with feathers on both sides.

21

Thinking and talking about flying giants

What is a pterosaur?

Which pterosaur ate insects?

What was the first bird?

Does this pterosaur have a long or short tail?

Which pterosaur was as big as a small aeroplane?

Activities

What did you think of this book?

 Brilliant   **Good**   **OK**

• • • • • • • • • • • •

Which of these flying giants was the biggest?

Pterodactylus • Quetzalcoatlus • Eudimorphodon

• • • • • • • • • • • •

Invent a flying giant. Draw a big picture and label it. Use these words:

tail • wings • jaws • crest

• • • • • • • • • • • •

Who is the author of this book?
Have you read *Dinosaur World Swimming Giants* by the same author?